Simple Machine Experiments

Using Seesaws, Wheels, Pulleys, and More

One Hour or Less Science Experiments

LAST MINUTE Science Projects

ROBERT GARDNER

Enslow Publishers, Inc.
40 Industrial Road
Box 398
Berkeley Heights, NJ 07922
USA

http://www.enslow.com

Library of Congress Cataloging-in-Publication Data

    Gardner, Robert, 1929–

    Simple machine experiments using seesaws, wheels, pulleys, and more : one hour or less science experiments / Robert Gardner.

    p. cm. — (Last-minute science projects)

    Includes bibliographical references and index.

    ISBN 978-0-7660-3957-5

    1. Machinery—Experiments—Juvenile literature. 2. Seesaw—Juvenile literature. 3. Wheels—Juvenile literature. 4. Pulleys—Juvenile literature. I. Title.

    TJ147.G364 2013

    621.8078—dc23

                           2011015586

Future editions

Paperback ISBN 978-1-4644-0142-8

ePUB ISBN 978-1-4645-1049-6

PDF ISBN 978-1-4646-1049-3

Printed in the United States of America

032012 Lake Book Manufacturing, Inc., Melrose Park, IL

10 9 8 7 6 5 4 3 2 1

To Our Readers: We have done our best to make sure all Internet Addresses in this book were active and appropriate when we went to press. However, the author and the publisher have no control over and assume no liability for the material available on those Internet sites or on other Web sites they may link to. Any comments or suggestions can be sent by e-mail to comments@enslow.com or to the address on the back cover.

♻ Enslow Publishers, Inc., is committed to printing our books on recycled paper. The paper in every book contains 10% to 30% post-consumer waste (PCW). The cover board on the outside of each book contains 100% PCW. Our goal is to do our part to help young people and the environment too!

Illustration Credits: © 2012 by Stephen Rountree (www.rountreegraphics.com), pp. 9, 11, 13, 15, 17 (b), 19 (a, b, d i), 21, 25, 27, 29, 35, 37, 41, 43; Tom LaBaff, pp. 17 (a), 19 (d ii, iii), 23, 31, 33, 39; Tom and Stephanie LaBaff, p. 19 (c); Shutterstock.com, pp. 1, 3, 4.

Contents

LAST MINUTE Science Projects

Contains ideas for more science fair projects.

Are You Running Late?

Do you have a science project due tomorrow and you've put it off until now? This book provides a solution! Here you will find experiments with simple machines that you can do in one hour or less. In fact, some of them can be done in 30 minutes, others in 15 minutes, and some in as little as 5 minutes. Even if you have plenty of time to prepare for your next science project or science fair, or if you are just looking for some fun science experiments, you can enjoy this book, too.

Most of the experiments are followed by a Keep Exploring section. There you will find ideas for projects or experiments in which the details are left to you. You can design and carry out your own experiments, **under adult supervision**, when you have more time.

Sometimes you may need a partner. Work with someone who likes to experiment as much as you do so you will both have fun. **Please follow any safety warnings and work with an adult when it is suggested**.

This is a book about simple machines. Machines are built to do work and to make work easier. Scientists define work as a force (a push or pull) times a distance. Work can be measured as a force, in pounds, times a distance, in feet. The product will be work measured in foot-pounds. In metric units, force times distance would be newtons times meters, so work would be in newton-meters, or joules. If possible, do Experiment 1. It will help you understand how to measure work.

The Scientific Method

Different sciences use different ways of experimenting. Depending on the problem, one method is likely to be better than another. Designing a new medicine for heart disease and finding evidence of water on Mars require different kinds of experiments.

Even with these differences, most scientists use the scientific method. This method includes making an observation, coming up with a question, making a hypothesis (a possible answer to the question) and a prediction (an if-then statement), designing and conducting an experiment, analyzing results, drawing conclusions, and deciding if the hypothesis is true or false. Scientists share their results. They publish articles in science journals.

Once you have a question, you can make a hypothesis. Your hypothesis is a possible answer to the question (what you think will happen). For example, you might hypothesize that pulling a weight up an inclined plane would be easier (require less force) than lifting the weight to the same height. Then you test your hypothesis.

In most cases you should do a controlled experiment. This means having two groups that are treated the same except for the thing being tested. That thing is called a variable. For example, to test the hypothesis above, you might have two identical objects. You would measure the force needed to lift one object as well as the force needed to pull the other up the inclined plane. If it took less force to pull the weight up the inclined plane, you would conclude that your hypothesis is true.

The results of one experiment often lead to another question. Or they may send you off in another direction. Whatever the results, something can be learned from every experiment!

Science Fairs

All of the investigations in this book contain ideas that might lead you to a science fair project. However, judges at science fairs do not reward projects or experiments that are simply copied from a book. For example, a diagram of a steam engine would not impress most judges; however, a balance made from a soda straw that could weigh the wing of a fly would attract their attention.

Science fair judges tend to reward creative thought and imagination. It is difficult to be creative or imaginative unless you are really interested in your project. Therefore, try to choose an investigation that excites you. And before you jump into a project, consider, too, your own talents and the cost of the materials you will need.

If you decide to use an experiment or idea found in this book for a science fair, find ways to modify or extend it. This should not be difficult. As you do investigations, you will get new ideas. You will think of questions that experiments can answer. The experiments will make great science fair projects because the ideas are your own and are interesting to you.

Your Notebook

Your notebook, as any scientist will tell you, is a valuable possession. It should contain ideas you may have as you experiment, sketches you may draw, calculations you make, and hypotheses you may suggest. It should include a description of every experiment you do, the data you record, such as weights, distances, and so on. It should also contain the results of your experiments, graphs you draw, and any conclusions you may be able to reach based on your results.

Safety First

1. Do any experiments or projects, whether from this book or of your own design, under the supervision of a science teacher or other knowledgeable adult. Do only those experiments that are described in the book or those that have been approved by an adult.

2. Read all instructions carefully before proceeding with a project. If you have questions, check with your supervisor before going any further.

3. Always wear safety goggles when doing experiments that could cause particles to enter your eyes. Tie back long hair. Wear shoes, not sandals.

4. Do not eat or drink while experimenting. Never taste substances being used (unless instructed to do so).

5. Do not touch chemicals, and do not let water drops fall on a hot lightbulb.

6. The liquid in some thermometers is mercury (a dense liquid metal). It is dangerous to touch mercury or breathe mercury vapor. Therefore, mercury thermometers have been banned in many states. When doing these experiments, use only non-mercury thermometers, such as those filled with alcohol. If you have a mercury thermometer in the house, ask an adult if it can be taken to a local thermometer exchange location.

7. Maintain a serious attitude while conducting experiments. Never engage in horseplay or play practical jokes.

8. Remove all items not needed for the experiment from your work space.

9. At the end of every activity, clean all materials used and put them away. Then wash your hands thoroughly with soap and water.

One Hour or Less

60 min

Here are experiments that you can do in one hour or less. If possible, do Experiment 1. It will show you how to measure work and friction, which are involved in all experiments with machines.

1 Measuring Work and Friction

What's the Plan?

Let's measure work and friction with and without machines.

What You Do

1. Fill a one-gallon jug with water. Put it in a cardboard box. Attach a loop of string to the box (Figure 1a). (You may have to make a hole in the box.)

2. Using a spring balance, pull the box 6 feet along a smooth floor. Pull parallel to the floor at a slow, steady speed. What force, in pounds, was needed to pull the box? Record that force. How much work did you do? (Remember: work equals force x distance.) If you pulled with a force of 5 pounds, the work you did was:

$$5 \text{ lbs} \times 6 \text{ ft} = 30 \text{ foot-pounds}$$

3. Put the box in a toy wagon. Using the spring balance, pull the wagon 6 feet along the same floor at a slow, steady speed (Figure 1b). What force was needed to pull the wagon? Record that force. How much work did you do?

WHAT YOU NEED:

- one-gallon jug
- water
- cardboard box
- string
- spring balance that can measure force in pounds
- yardstick
- toy wagon
- notebook
- pen or pencil

What's Going On?

When you pulled the box at a constant speed, your force equaled the force of friction that opposed the motion. If your force was greater than friction, the box would have accelerated. So the work you did, which was your pulling force times 6 feet, was the work needed to overcome friction.

The wagon consists of several simple machines (wheels and axles). Even though the wagon and box weighed more than the box alone, less work was needed. The machines reduced friction and, therefore, the work needed to move the box.

Keep Exploring—If You Have More Time!

- Suppose, instead of pulling the box with a force parallel to the floor, you pull upward at an angle to the floor. Will the force needed to move the box change? Why or why not?

a)

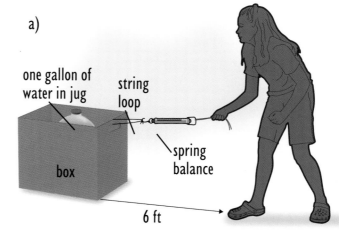

b)

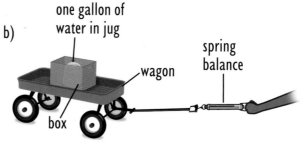

Figure 1. a) Pull a box 6 feet along a smooth floor. How much work is done? b) Put the box in a toy wagon. Pull the wagon 6 feet along the same floor. How much work is done?

2 A First-Class Lever

What's the Plan?

Let's investigate a first-class lever. A lever is a rod that turns on a pivot (the fulcrum) and may be used to lift weights. A first-class lever has the fulcrum between the load (L) to be moved and the force (F) used to move the load (Figure 2a).

WHAT YOU NEED:
• small piece of wood
• clay
• table
• tape
• string
• yardstick
• spring balance
• hammer
• notebook
• pen or pencil
• a partner

What You Do

1. Make a fulcrum from a piece of wood. Use clay to secure the wood near one corner of a table. The clay can be used to tip the wood, forming a pivot line on which the lever can turn (Figure 2b).

2. Using tape, fasten a loop of string to each end of a yardstick.

3. Using a spring balance, weigh a hammer. Record its weight.

4. Ask a partner to help assemble the lever. Place the 12-inch line of the lever (yardstick) on the fulcrum. Hang the hammer from the 0-inch end of the lever.

5. Attach the spring balance to the 36-inch end of the lever (Figure 2c). Using the spring balance, find the force needed to lift the load (hammer). Record that force.

6. Repeat the experiment with the fulcrum at the 6-inch line. What force will lift the load now?

What's Going On?

With the fulcrum at the 12-inch line, the force to lift the load was approximately half as much as the load's weight. The force you applied was twice as far from the fulcrum as the load. Taking into account some friction, you will find that the weight of the load (L) times its distance (d) from the fulcrum equals the force (F) times its distance (D) from the fulcrum ($L \times d = F \times D$).

Keep Exploring—If You Have More Time!

- Show that the work done on the load (L) is approximately equal to the work done by the lifting force.

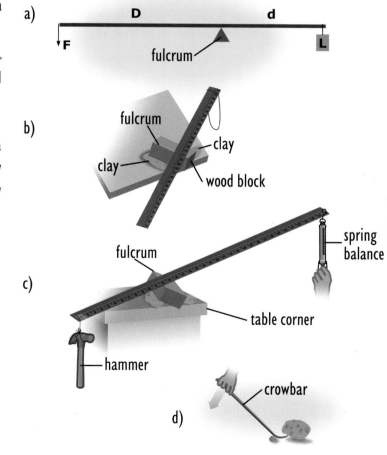

Figure 2. a) A first-class lever
b) Make a fulcrum.
c) A working first-class lever
d) A crowbar is a useful first-class lever for moving heavy objects.

3 Double Pulley: A Simple Machine

What's the Plan?
Let's see how a double pulley makes work easier.

What You Do

1. Ask a partner to help you arrange the two-pulley machine shown in Figure 3a. Begin at the place labeled one (1). Tie the end of the string to a hook or opening at the bottom of the pulley.

2. Thread the string as shown—1, 2, 3, 4, 5.

3. Using a spring balance, measure the weight of an object, such as a hammer, that you plan to lift with the pulleys. Record the object's weight.

4. Use string to attach the object to the bottom pulley.

5. Connect a spring balance to the end of the string at position 5.

6. Use the spring balance to measure the force needed to (a) balance the weight; and (b) slowly raise the weight.

WHAT YOU NEED:

- a partner
- string
- hook
- 2 pulleys, one with two wheels
- spring balance
- weight, such as a hammer
- pen or pencil
- notebook

What's Going On?
With the double pulley threaded as shown, there are four strings balancing the load. The force is distributed among the four strings lifting the weight.

Therefore, the upward-balancing force recorded on the spring scale should be about one-fourth the downward-pulling weight plus the weight of the pulley. When you raised the weight with the spring balance, the force probably increased because of friction in the pulleys.

Keep Exploring—If You Have More Time!

Investigate other multiple pulley systems such as those shown in Figure 3b.

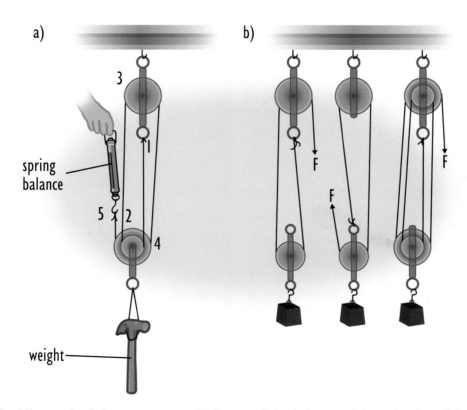

Figure 3. a) Use a spring balance to measure the force needed to balance and then raise the weight.
b) Investigate other double pulley systems. The force, F, shows where the lifting force is applied with a spring scale. Knowing the weight to be lifted, can you predict the approximate force needed to lift it?

4 A Complex Machine

What's the Plan?

Let's build and run a complex machine made from two simple machines—an inclined plane and a pulley.

What You Do

1. Place one end of a long (5 feet or more), wide board against the seat of a chair or low table. The other end can rest on the floor.

2. Tape some weights, such as large wood blocks, to a toy truck. Use a spring balance to weigh the loaded truck. Record its weight.

3. Use the spring balance to measure the force needed to pull the truck slowly up the inclined plane (Figure 4a). Record the force.

4. Ask a partner to help you attach a single pulley to the truck resting at the bottom of the incline. Run a string through the pulley. Hold one end of the string at the top of the incline. Connect the other end of the string to a spring balance.

5. Use the spring balance and pulley to slowly pull the truck up the incline (Figure 4b). How much force is needed to pull the truck up the inclined plane? Record the force. How do the two forces compare?

WHAT YOU NEED:

- long (5 feet or more), wide board
- chair or low table
- weights, such as large wood blocks
- tape
- toy truck
- spring balance
- pencil and notebook
- a partner
- single pulley
- string

What's Going On?

The inclined plane made it easier to pull the truck up to the chair than to lift the truck to the same height. By adding a single pulley, the force needed was even less. Ideally, the pulley, as shown, would have made the force half as large. However, friction in the pulley probably made the force a little more than half as much.

Keep Exploring—If You Have More Time!

- Add a third machine, such as a wheel and axle, to the inclined plane and the pulley. How much will the third machine change the force needed to pull the truck up the incline?

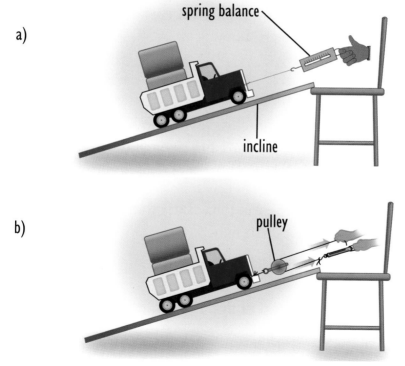

Figure 4. a) What force is needed to pull the truck up the inclined plane?
b) Using two machines, an inclined plane and a pulley, what force is needed to pull the truck up the incline?

30 Minutes or Less

Really pressed for time? Here are some experiments you can do in 30 minutes or less.

5 A Second-Class Lever

WHAT YOU NEED:
- yardstick
- a partner
- tape
- table or bench
- string
- spring balance
- hammer
- pencil and notebook

What's the Plan?

Let's investigate a second-class lever. A lever is a rod or bar that turns on a pivot (fulcrum) and is used to move weights. A second-class lever has both the load (L) to be moved and the force (F) lifting the load on the same side of the fulcrum (Figure 5a). To make work easier, the load should be close to the fulcrum.

What You Do

1. You'll use a yardstick as a second-class lever. Have a partner keep the zero end of the yardstick against the surface near the end of a table or bench. That end of the yardstick will be the lever's fulcrum.

2. Using tape, fasten a loop of string to the other end of the yardstick. Fasten another loop at the 12-inch line.

3. Using a spring balance, weigh a hammer. Record its weight.

4. Hang the hammer from the loop at the 12-inch mark.

5. Attach the spring balance to the end of the yardstick (Figure 5b). Use the spring balance to find the force needed to lift the load (hammer). Record that force.

6. Repeat the experiment with the hammer at the 6-inch line. What force lifts the load now?

What's Going On?

With the hammer at the 12-inch line, the force to lift the load was about one-third the load's weight. The force you applied was three times as far from the fulcrum as the load. You will find that the load (L) times its distance (d) from the fulcrum approximately equals the force (F) times its distance (D) from the fulcrum, or $L \times d = F \times D$.

Keep Exploring—If You Have More Time!

- Show that the work done on the load (L) about equals the work done by the lifting force.

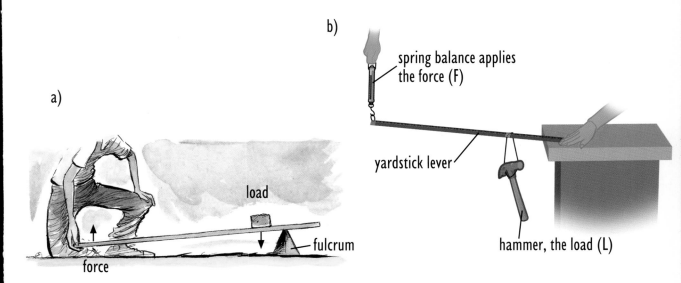

Figure 5. a) A second-class lever b) A setup for a second-class lever

6 A Third-Class Lever

WHAT YOU NEED:
- yardstick
- a partner
- table
- tape
- string
- spring balance
- hammer
- pen or pencil
- notebook

What's the Plan?

Let's investigate a third-class lever. A third-class lever has both the load (L) to be lifted and the force (F) used to lift the load on the same side of the fulcrum (f) (Figure 6a). The load is farther from the fulcrum than the lifting force, which makes work difficult.

What You Do

1 We'll use a yardstick as a third-class lever. Have a partner keep one end of the yardstick against the surface of a table near the table's edge. That end of the yardstick will be the fulcrum.

2. Tape a loop of string to the other end of the yardstick. Fasten another loop 12 inches from that end of the yardstick.

3. Using a spring balance, weigh a hammer. Record its weight. Then hang the hammer from the loop at the end of the yardstick.

4. Attach the spring balance to the loop that is 12 inches from the yardstick's end (Figure 6b). Use the spring balance to find the force needed to lift the load (hammer). Record that force.

5. Repeat the experiment with the spring balance 6 inches from the loop supporting the hammer. What force lifts the load now?

What's Going On?

With the hammer at the lever's end, the force to lift the load was about 1.5 times as much as the load's weight. The force you applied was 2/3 as far from the fulcrum as the load. You will find that the load (L) times its distance (D) from the fulcrum approximately equals the force (F) times its distance (d) from the fulcrum, or L x D = F x d (Figure 6c).

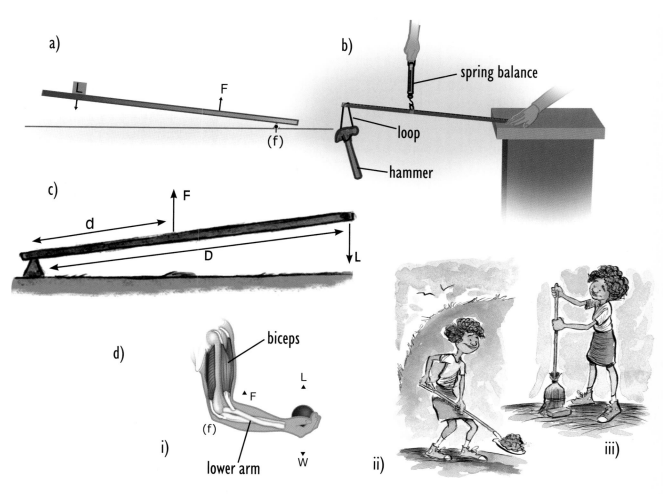

Figure 6 a) A third-class lever does not make work easier. b) A working third-class lever c) L x D = F x d d) Some third-class levers: (i) a human arm; (ii) a shovel; (iii) a broom

7 The Seesaw, a First-Class Lever

What's the Plan?

Why is a seesaw a first-class lever? A lever is a bar that turns on a pivot (fulcrum) and is used to move weights. A first-class lever has the fulcrum between the weight (W_1) to be lifted and the force (W_2) used to lift the weight (Figure 7a).

What You Do

1. Find a playground with a seesaw. Sit on one side of the seesaw. Have a partner who is about your size sit on the other side. The seesaw will balance because your weight (W_1) makes the seesaw turn one way. Your partner's weight (W_2) makes the seesaw turn the other way.

2. Ask an adult who is heavier than you to sit on the other side of the seesaw. The seesaw on the adult's side will go down and you will go up.

3. To make the seesaw balance, ask the adult to move closer to the fulcrum (Figure 7b). Or you may be able to balance the seesaw by moving the board so that so that you are farther from the fulcrum than the adult (Figure 7c).

What's Going On?

The seesaw is a first-class lever because the fulcrum is between the weight to be lifted (W_1) and the force (W_2) used to lift W_1. For a seesaw to balance, W_1 x its distance from the fulcrum (D_1) must equal the weight on the other side (W_2) x its distance from the fulcrum (D_2). That is, for balance, $W_1 \times D_1 = W_2 \times D_2$. Balance can be achieved either by moving weights or by changing the position of the fulcrum (the point around which the seesaw turns).

Keep Exploring—If You Have More Time!

- Figure out ways to balance a seesaw when more than two people are sitting on it.

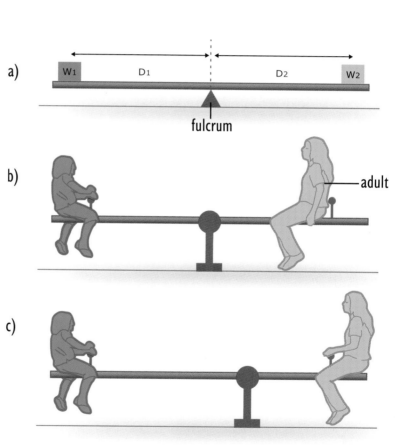

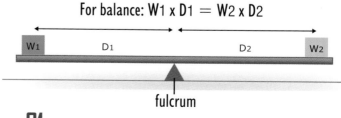

Figure 7. a) A first-class lever
b) With a heavier person, balance can be achieved by having the heavier person sit closer to the fulcrum.
c) Or the lighter person can sit farther from the fulcrum.
d) For balance: $W_1 \times D_1 = W_2 \times D_2$

8 An Inclined Plane: Another Simple Machine

What's the Plan?
Let's investigate the inclined plane.

What You Do

WHAT YOU NEED:
- weights, such as large wood blocks
- toy truck
- tape
- spring balance
- long (5 feet or more), wide board
- books or low table
- yardstick
- pen or pencil
- notebook

1. Tape some weights, such as large wood blocks, to a toy truck. Use a spring balance to weigh the loaded truck (Figure 8a).

2. Place one end of a long (5 feet or more), wide board on a pile of books or low table. The other end can rest on the floor.

3. Measure the distance from the floor to the top of the books or tabletop.

4. How much work is done lifting the loaded truck from the floor to the top of the books or table? (Remember, work = force x distance.)

5. Measure the force needed to pull the loaded truck along the inclined plane (Figure 8b).

6. Calculate the work required to move the truck along the inclined plane from the floor to the top of the books or table.

7. Turn the loaded truck upside down. Then measure the force needed to pull it along the inclined plane.

What's Going On?

The force to move the truck along the inclined plane was less than the force to lift it (its weight). However, the smaller force had to act over a longer distance when you pulled the truck up the inclined plane. Therefore, you may have done more work pulling it along the incline than lifting it straight up from floor to table. Although more work may be required—especially if the weight is dragged, not rolled—it is usually easier to pull it along the incline than to lift it straight up.

Keep Exploring—If You Have More Time!

- How does the angle of the incline affect the force used to move the truck up the inclined plane?

- How can you reduce the force needed to pedal your bike up a steep hill?

a)

spring
balance

**Figure 8. a) Use a spring balance to weigh a loaded toy truck.
b) What force is needed to pull the truck up the inclined plane?
How much work is done?**

b)

9 The Wheel and Axle: Another Simple Machine

What's the Plan?

Let's investigate a wheel and axle and see how it makes work easier.

What You Do

WHAT YOU NEED:
- spring scale
- weight such as a hammer
- pen or pencil
- notebook
- bicycle
- string

1. Using a spring scale, weigh an object such as a hammer. Record its weight.

2. Turn a bicycle upside down. Using string, attach the weight to the middle of a spoke (Figure 9a).

3. Using another string, attach a spring scale to the tire tread.

4. Use the spring scale to find the force needed to raise the weight attached to the spoke. You'll find the force is about half the weight of the object hanging from the spoke.

5. Move the weight closer to the wheel's axle. The force needed to raise the weight becomes less.

6. Move the weight farther from the axle. The force needed to raise the weight becomes larger.

What's Going On?

A wheel and axle is similar to a first-class lever (Figure 9b). It makes work easier. If the weight is attached to the axle, one turn of the wheel raises the weight a very short distance. Your force (measured by the spring scale) on the wheel's circumference was smaller than the weight lifted. But your force moved a large distance, while the weight moved a small distance.

You used a small force (f) over a large distance (D) to pull on the wheel. The work you did was about the same as the work done on the weight (W), which moved a small distance (d).

f	x	D	=	W	x	d
your small force on wheel		large distance force moved		large weight		small distance weight moved

A small force applied to the wheel's circumference can lift a heavy object attached to the axle.

Keep Exploring—If You Have More Time!

- Show how a hand-turned pencil sharpener is a simple machine that makes work easier.

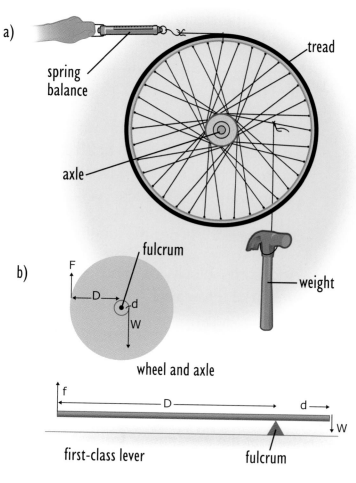

a)

tread

spring balance

axle

b)

fulcrum

F

D

d

W

weight

wheel and axle

f

D

d

W

first-class lever

fulcrum

Figure 9. a) Measure the force to raise a weight using a wheel and axle.
b) A wheel and axle is similar to a first-class lever.

25

15 Minutes or Less

15 min

Time is really in short supply if you need an experiment you can do in 15 minutes. Here to rescue you are more experiments you can do quickly.

10 What Is the Effect of an Inclined Plane's Steepness?

What's the Plan?

How does the steepness of an inclined plane affect the ease of doing work?

What You Do

WHAT YOU NEED:
- large protractor
- long inclined plane (board)
- blocks or books
- ruler or yardstick
- toy truck
- pen or pencil
- notebook
- blocks or books
- spring balance

1. Use a large protractor to set the angle of an inclined plane (board) at 20 degrees (Figure 10a). Blocks or books can be placed under the upper end of the board to adjust the angle.

2. Measure and record the length of the inclined plane.

3. Add some blocks or other objects to increase the weight of a toy truck.

4. Using a spring balance, measure the force needed to pull the toy truck up the inclined plane (Figure 10b). Calculate the work you did to pull the truck up the inclined plane. Multiply the force times the distance you pulled the truck.

5. Repeat the experiment for inclined-plane angles of 40, 60, and 80 degrees.

What's Going On?

Increasing the angle of the inclined plane increased the force needed to pull the truck up the incline. For angles greater than 60 degrees, the force needed to pull the truck was nearly as large as the truck's weight. The work you did in each experiment equals the force with which you pulled the truck times the distance you pulled it (the length of the incline).

Keep Exploring—If You Have More Time!

- Do an experiment to show that because of friction, the force needed to drag a heavy object up a steep incline may be greater than the object's weight.

- Do an experiment to show how the angle of an incline affects the final speed of a ball that rolls down the incline.

- Make a graph of the force needed to pull the truck up the incline vs. angle. Use it to predict the angle at which the force to pull the truck would be half the force to lift the truck.

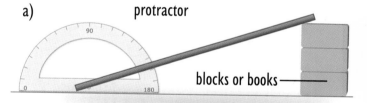

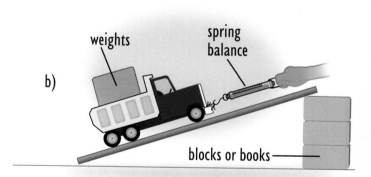

Figure 10. a) Use a protractor to establish the angle of an inclined plane. b) Use a spring balance to measure the force needed to pull a toy truck up the inclined plane.

11 Screws and Bolts: Modified Inclined Planes

What's the Plan?
Why are screws and bolts inclined planes?

What You Do

1. Cut out a paper triangle 12 inches long and 6 inches high (Figure 11a).

2. Starting with the wide end, wind the paper around a pencil. As you can see, a very thin inclined plane is now spiraled around the pencil. Screws and bolts are inclined planes wound around a cylinder.

3. Let's see how the angle of a screw's inclined plane affects the force needed to turn the screw. Find two screws of about the same diameter. One screw should have the threads much closer together than the other (Figure 11b).

4. Using a screwdriver, screw each screw, in turn, into a piece of wood. You'll find it much easier to turn the screw with the threads closer together.

WHAT YOU NEED:
- paper
- ruler
- pencil
- 2 screws, one with threads close together, one with threads farther apart
- screwdriver
- piece of wood
- scissors

What's Going On?
The threads on a screw or bolt are a continuous inclined plane. The farther apart the threads, the steeper the incline. Much like a hill, the steeper the incline, the harder it is to move up the incline. You found this to be true. It was harder to turn the screw with threads far apart than with threads close together.

Keep Exploring—If You Have More Time!

- Do an experiment to compare the work done in making one turn of a closely threaded screw with the work done to turn a screw in which the threads are farther apart.

- Do a similar experiment to compare the work done on a closely threaded bolt with one that has fewer threads per inch.

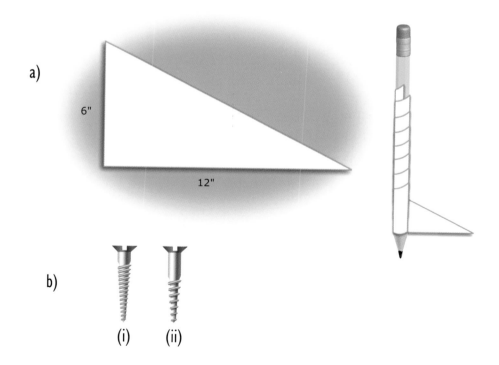

Figure 11. a) A screw is a narrow inclined plane wound around a cylinder.
b) Two screws of similar size: (i) many threads per inch, (ii) fewer threads per inch

12 A Single Pulley

What's the Plan?

Let's use a fixed single pulley and then a movable single pulley to lift a weight.

What You Do

WHAT YOU NEED:
- single pulley
- hook
- spring balance
- pail
- pen or pencil
- notebook
- strong string

1. Attach a single pulley to a hook.

2. Use a spring balance to weigh a pail. Record that weight.

3. Tie a strong string to the pail's handle. Run the string over the fixed pulley.

4. Use the spring balance to pull down on the string and lift the load (Figure 12a). Record the force needed to raise the pail.

5. Connect the pulley to the pail with string or a hook. Connect a string to a hook. Run the string through the pulley so you can lift the load with the moveble pulley. Use the spring scale to measure the force needed to raise the load with the movable pulley (Figure 12b).

What's Going On?

As you found, it takes more force to lift the load using the fixed pulley than to lift it by hand. The reason is that there is friction in the pulley that has to be overcome. The reason for using a fixed pulley is so that you can pull down instead of up. Pulling down is less likely to strain your back than pulling up.

When you used the movable pulley, both sides of the string were lifting the load. Ideally, this should make your force half as large as the weight lifted. But, again, there is friction in the pulley so the lifting force is a bit more than half the pail's weight.

Keep Exploring—If You Have More Time!

- Do an experiment to show that for both a fixed and a moveable pulley the work you do is greater than the work done on the weight. (Remember, work = force x distance.)

Figure 12. a) Use a fixed pulley to lift a weight. b) Use a movable pulley to lift a weight. The string on one side of the movable pulley provides half the force to lift the weight; the string on the other side provides the other half.

31

13 Bearings Reduce Friction

What's the Plan?

How do ball bearings make the wheel and axle more efficient?

What You Do

WHAT YOU NEED:

• toy wagon

• spring scale

• 2 one-gallon cans of paint

• about 10 identical marbles

1. Turn a toy wagon upside down. Pull it using a spring scale. How much force is needed?

2. Turn the wagon right-side up so it can roll on its wheels. Again, pull it with the spring scale. How much force is needed this time? As you can see, rolling friction is much less than sliding friction.

3. To reduce friction between a wheel and the axle on which it turns, ball bearings are used. To see why, place a full one-gallon can of paint on top of an identical can (Figure 13a). Notice how hard it is to turn the upper can on the lower can.

4. Now place about 10 identical marbles along the rim of the lower can (Figure 13b). Then replace the upper can. The marbles work like ball bearings. Try turning the upper can again. Do the bearings make it easier to turn the can?

What's Going On?

Friction always acts against motion. But, as you saw, rolling friction is much less than sliding friction. Ball bearings, which are usually made of steel balls, not marbles, reduce friction between a wheel and its axle. The bearings change sliding friction to rolling friction. So adding ball bearings to wheels makes the wheel and axle a very efficient machine.

Keep Exploring—If You Have More Time!

- Do an experiment to show that you can't walk without friction.

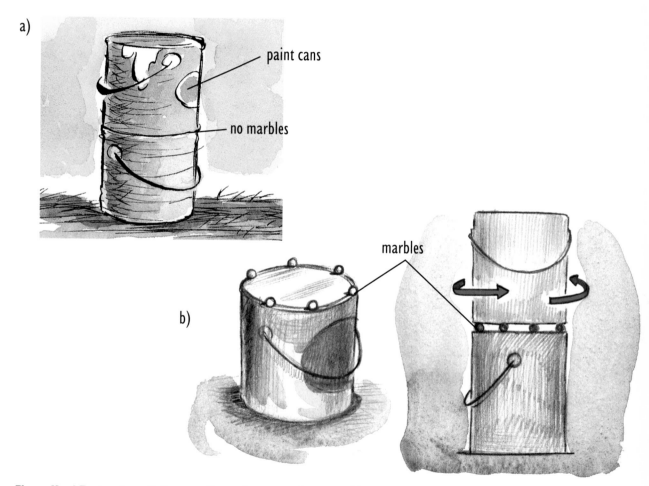

a)

paint cans

no marbles

marbles

b)

Figure 13. a) Try turning a full one-gallon paint can resting on an identical can. b) Place identical marbles along the rim of a full one-gallon paint can. Put an identical can of paint on the "ball bearings." How difficult is it to turn the upper can now?

5 Minutes or Less

Are you desperate? Do you have very little time to prepare a project? If so, you have come to the right place. Here are experiments you can do in five minutes or less.

14 Using a Lever to Control Motion

What's the Plan?

Let's use a lever to prevent a motion. A lever is a rod or bar that turns on a pivot (the fulcrum) and is used to lift weights and move things. A second-class lever, like the one used here (Figure 14a), has the load (L) to be controlled and the controlling force (F) on the same side of the fulcrum. To make the controlling work easier, the force (F) is farther from the fulcrum than the load (L).

WHAT YOU NEED:
- long-handled broom
- strong person
- small piece of paper

What You Do

1. Give a long-handled broom to a strong person. That person is to hold the broom's handle with both hands together near the straw part of the broom (Figure 14b).

2. Tell that person to try to put the end of the handle on a small piece of paper you have put on the floor as a target.

3. Using a single finger near the end of the broom handle, your small force can prevent the stronger person from touching the target with the broom's handle.

What's Going On?

By experiment, you can show that at equilibrium the load (L) times its distance (d) from the fulcrum equals your force (F) times its distance (D) from the fulcrum, or L x d = F x D. Since your force is so much farther from the fulcrum than the strong person's, you can easily overcome any force he or she applies to the other end of the broom handle.

Keep Exploring—If You Have More Time!

- Build an equal-arm balance using a yardstick, nails, paper clips, string, paper plates, a means of support, and whatever else you think is needed. How accurately can you weigh objects on your balance? Can you weigh to ± 0.1 g? To ± 0.01 g?

- Can you build a balance that can weigh a fly? A fly's wing?

a)

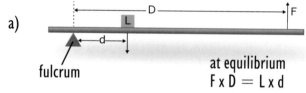

at equilibrium
$F \times D = L \times d$

Figure 14. a) A second-class lever: Both the load and the applied force lifting the load are on the same side of the fulcrum. The work is made easier because the lifting force is farther from the fulcrum than the load. b) A broom can serve as a lever. It will allow a small person to control the strength of a large, strong person.

b)

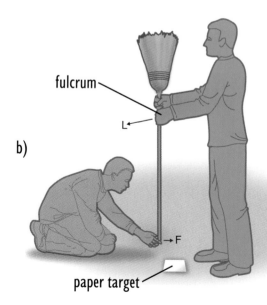

15 A Simple Multiple-Pulley System

What's the Plan?

Let's make a simple multiple-pulley system.

What You Do

1. Tie a long length of clothesline to a sturdy wooden dowel. Place the dowel near a second identical dowel.

2. Wrap the clothesline six or seven times around the two dowels, as shown in Figure 15.

3. Invite two strong people to try to keep the dowels apart while you pull on the free end of the clothesline.

What's Going On?

Doubling the number of loops around the dowels doubles the force that you can use to pull the dowels together. With four loops, you can pull the dowels together with twice as much force as the two people (assuming all have equal strength) can pull them apart.

Keep Exploring—If You Have More Time!

• Compare the force needed to lift a weight using this simple multiple pulley system with a real pulley system having as many supporting strands. Why is the simple system less efficient than the one using real pulleys?

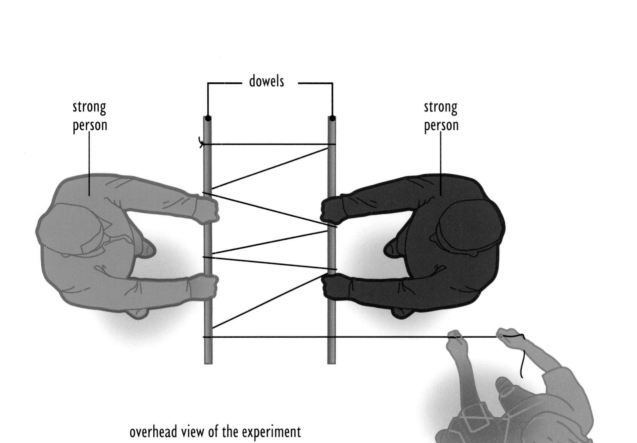

dowels

strong
person

strong
person

overhead view of the experiment

you

Figure 15. How many loops are needed for you to pull the dowels together?

16 The Wedge: A Two-Sided Inclined Plane

What's the Plan?

How can the wedge, a simple machine, make work easier? A wedge is a two-sided inclined plane. Objects do not move up the wedge. It is the wedge that moves.

WHAT YOU NEED:

• 3-inch x 5-inch file card

• ruler and tape

• heavy cardboard

What You Do

1. You can make a small wedge. Fold a 3-inch x 5-inch file card in half, as shown in Figure 16a.

2. Fold 1/2 inch of each end of the card inward as shown.

3. Tape these folded ends together. You have made a small wedge.

4. Using your wedge, lift a piece of heavy cardboard. Slowly push the wedge under the cardboard (Figure 16b). Push until you have raised the cardboard as high as the wedge allows.

What's Going On?

Wedges are moving inclined planes. A wedge, like an ax, moving into something creates a force sideways to its motion. When an ax strikes a log, it pushes the wood apart.

A small force on the wedge you made lifted a heavy piece of cardboard half an inch (the thickness of the wedge). You moved the wedge two inches, the cardboard rose 1/2 inch (the maximum thickness of the wedge).

Like other simple machines, a small force on the wedge put a large force on the load (cardboard). The small force on the wedge moved the wedge two inches. The heavier load (the cardboard) moved only 1/2 inch. Your work on the wedge was about the same as the work done on the cardboard.

f	x	D	=	F	x	d
small force on wedge		large distance force moved		large force to lift cardboard		small distance cardboard was lifted

a)

2½"

3"

½"

½"

tape

b)

cardboard   wedge

Figure 16 a) Make a wedge from a 3-inch by 5-inch file card. b) Use the wedge to lift a cardboard sheet. The wedge moves 2 inches to lift the cardboard 1/2 inch.

17 A Lever Is for Lifting

Do this experiment under adult supervision.

What's the Plan?

Let's see how a lever can make work easier.

What You Do

1. Find a heavy table or desk. Try to lift one end of the table or desk. You should find it difficult or impossible.

2. Place a 2 x 4 on end next to the table or desk. Its upper end should be at about the same height as the tabletop (Figure 17a).

3. Place a second slightly longer 2 x 4 on top of the first 2 x 4. Wrap one of its ends with a cloth. Place that end under the table or desktop. The top of the vertical 2 x 4 will serve as a fulcrum for your lever.

WHAT YOU NEED:

- an adult

- heavy table or desk

- cloth to protect table

- 2 x 4 wooden board about as long as the height of the table or desk

- second 2 x 4 slightly longer than the first

4. Push down on the opposite end of the 2 x 4 that is under the tabletop (Figure 17b). You will find that you can lift the table quite easily.

What's Going On?

You made a first-class lever. A lever is a rod or bar that turns on a pivot (the fulcrum) and can be used to lift weights. A first-class lever has the fulcrum

40

between the load (L) to be lifted and the force (F) used to lift the load (Figure 17c). At equilibrium, the load (table or desk) times its distance (d) from the fulcrum equals the force (F) you applied to the end of the lever times its distance (D) from the fulcrum, or L x d = F x D. Actually, to lift a load, F x D must be slightly larger than L x d because of friction on the fulcrum that you have to overcome.

Keep Exploring—If You Have More Time!

- Invent a lever that can be used to test the strength of various types of thread.

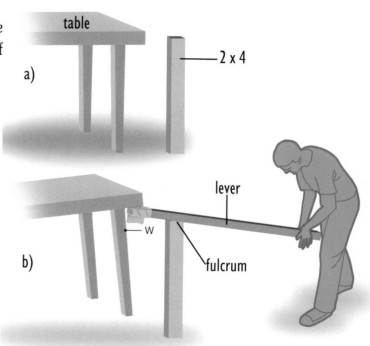

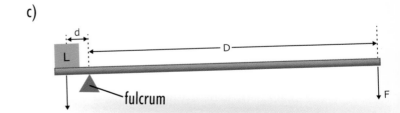

Figure 17. a) Find a 2 x 4 that has a length approximately the same as the height of a heavy table or desk. b) Use a longer 2 x 4 as a lever to lift the heavy table or desk. Use the end of the vertical 2 x 4 as a fulcrum. c) A first-class lever has a load, L, on one side of the fulcrum and a lifting force, F, on the other side. At equilibrium, L x d = F x D.

18 Why Are Doorknobs on the Side Opposite the Hinges?

What's the Plan?

Let's see why a door is like a lever and find the easy and the hard way to close a door.

WHAT YOU NEED:

- an adult
- tape
- cloth
- spring balance
- door
- kitchen stool

What You Do

1. Tape a piece of cloth to the hook at the end of a spring balance. This will protect the door you will move with the spring balance.

2. Using the spring balance, move a door by pulling on the side opposite the hinges (Figure 18a). How much force is needed to move the door?

3. Place a kitchen stool near the door's hinged side. Under adult supervision, stand on the stool. Use the spring balance to pull on the door near the top of the hinged side (Figure 18b). How much force is needed here to move the door?

What's Going On?

A door is like a lever. We can consider all the door's weight (its center of gravity) to be at its center and its fulcrum to be the hinges. By pulling on the doorknob or any point on the side of the door opposite the hinges, we have something similar to a second-class lever (Figure 18c). A lever is a rod that turns on a pivot (the fulcrum) and is used to move heavy objects.

A second-class lever has the load (L) to be moved between the fulcrum and the force (F) used to move the load. By having the force farther from the fulcrum than the load, a small force can move a larger load.

Placing the force closer to the fulcrum (hinges) than the load makes it harder to move the load. So you can see why doorknobs are placed on the side of the door opposite the hinges.

Keep Exploring—If You Have More Time!

- What kind of simple machine is a doorknob? How about a latch-type door closer?

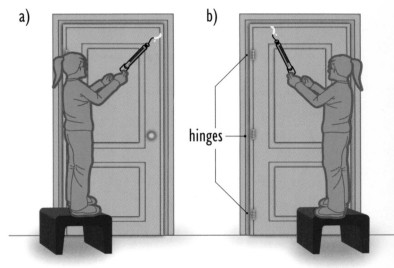

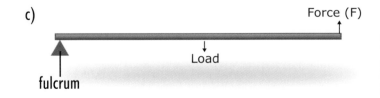

Figure 18. a) How much force is needed to move the door if you pull on the side opposite the hinges? b) How much force is needed if you pull on the hinged side of the door? c) A second-class lever

Words to Know

ball bearings—Friction-reducing, hard metal balls against which a rotating shaft or other part can turn.

bolt—A narrow inclined plane wound around a central cylindrical core. The steeper the incline, the fewer the number of threads per centimeter.

complex machine—A machine consisting of two or more simple machines.

first-class lever—A lever in which the fulcrum is between the load and the force used to lift it.

force—A push or a pull, often measured in pounds or newtons.

friction—A force that opposes the movement of an object.

fulcrum—A pivot about which a lever turns.

inclined plane—A simple machine consisting of a plane, such as a board, raised at one end. If friction is small, less force is needed to move an object up the incline than to lift it to the same height.

lever—A simple machine consisting of a rod or bar that turns on a pivot (fulcrum) and is used to lift or move weights.

multiple-pulley system—A simple machine consisting of two or more pulleys.

pulley—A simple machine consisting of one or more wheels and a rope that can be used to raise weights or change the direction of a force.

screw—A narrow inclined plane spiraled around a cylinder. The steeper the incline, the fewer the number of threads per inch.

second-class lever—A lever in which the load is between the fulcrum and the lifting force.

seesaw—A first-class lever, often found on playgrounds, that consists of a plank that rests on a central fulcrum.

simple machine—A device that makes work easier or changes the direction of force.

spring balance—A spring that has been calibrated to measure forces. A spring balance works because doubling the force on a spring doubles the spring's length.

steepness—A relative measure of the angle of an incline. The greater the angle, the steeper the incline.

third-class lever—A lever in which the lifting force is between the fulcrum and the load.

wedge—A two-sided inclined plane.

weight—The force exerted on a mass by Earth's gravity.

wheel and axle—A simple machine that makes work easier. A small force applied to the wheel can lift a much larger force (weight) attached to the axle. It is similar to a first-class lever.

work—The product of a force and the distance through which the force acts.

Further Reading

Armentrout, David and Patricia. *Wedges*. Vero Beach, Fla.: Rourke Publishing, 2009.

Bardhan-Quallen, Sudipta. *Championship Science Fair Projects: 100 Sure-to-Win Experiments*. New York: Sterling, 2009.

Bochinski, Julianne Blair. *More Award-Winning Science Fair Projects*. Hoboken, N.J.:, John Wiley and Sons, 2004.

DiSpezio, Michael A. *Super Sensational Science Fair Projects*. New York: Sterling, 2004.

Howse, Jennifer. *Inclined Planes*. New York: Weigl Publishers, 2010.

———. *Levers*. New York: Weigl Publishers, 2010.

Oxlade, Chris. *Wedges and Ramps*. Mankato, Minn.: Smart Apple Media, 2009.

———.*Wheels*. Mankato, Minn.: Smart Apple Media, 2003.

Rhatigan, Joe, and Rain Newcomb. *Prize-Winning Science Fair Projects for Curious Kids*. New York: Lark Books, 2006.

Thompson, Gare. *Lever, Screw, and Inclined Plane: The Power of Simple Machines*. Washington, D.C.: National Geographic, 2006.

Internet Addresses

Science Fair Projects & Games to Download
  <http://www.kids-online-games.com/>

Simple Machines
  <http://42explore.com/smplmac.htm>

Index